GW01086875

STILL MORE ANTONYMS

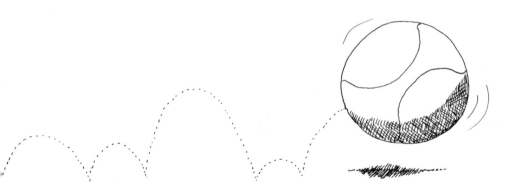

together and apart and other
WORDS THAT ARE AS DIFFERENT IN
MEANING
as rise and fall

STILL MORE ANTONYMS

JOAN HANSON

Published by
Lerner Publications Company
Minneapolis, Minnesota

International Standard Book Number: 0-8225-1106-1
Library of Congress Catalog Card Number: 76-22421

3 4 5 6 7 8 9 10 85 84 83 82 81 80 79

an·to·nym (AN-tuh-nim) A word that means the opposite of another word. The antonym of *hard* is *soft*. *Tall* is the antonym of *short*.

Rise

POP!

Fall

Together

Apart

Firm

Shaky

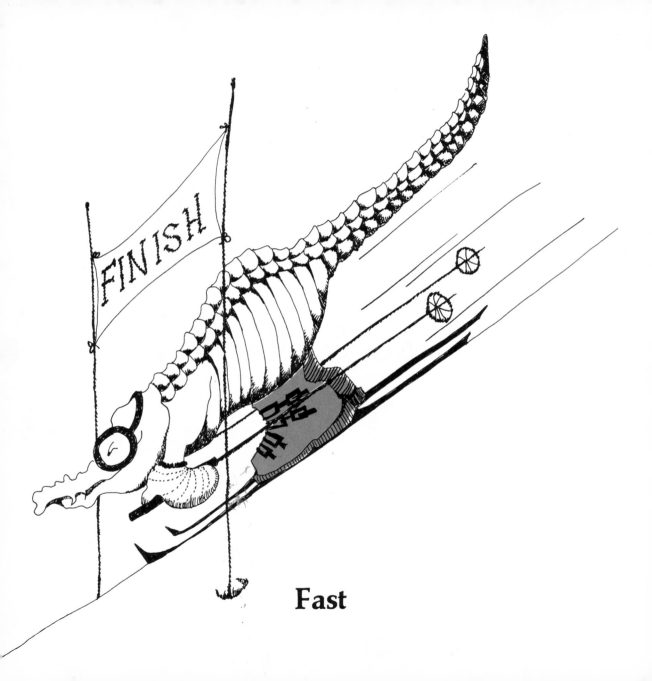

Fast

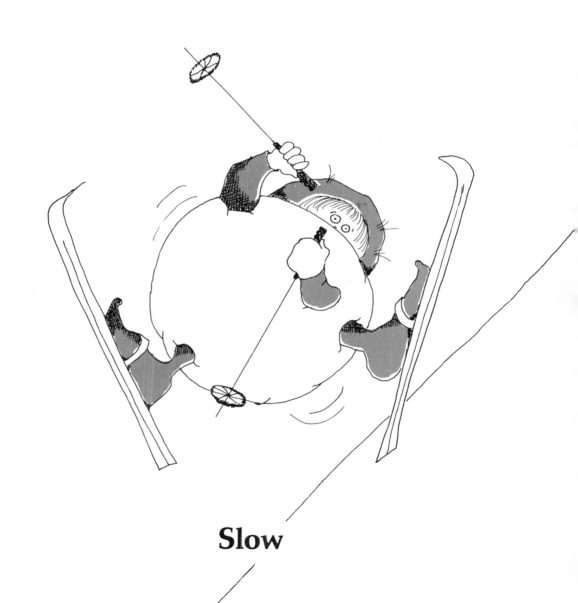

Slow

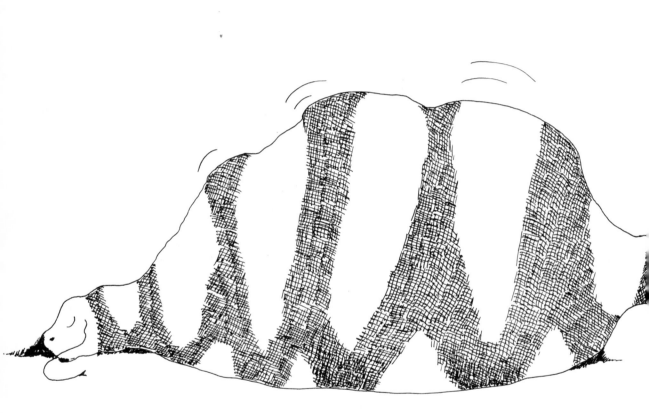

Thick

Thin

Quiet

Noisy

Tight

Loose

Careless

Careful

Happy

Sad

Shy

Bold

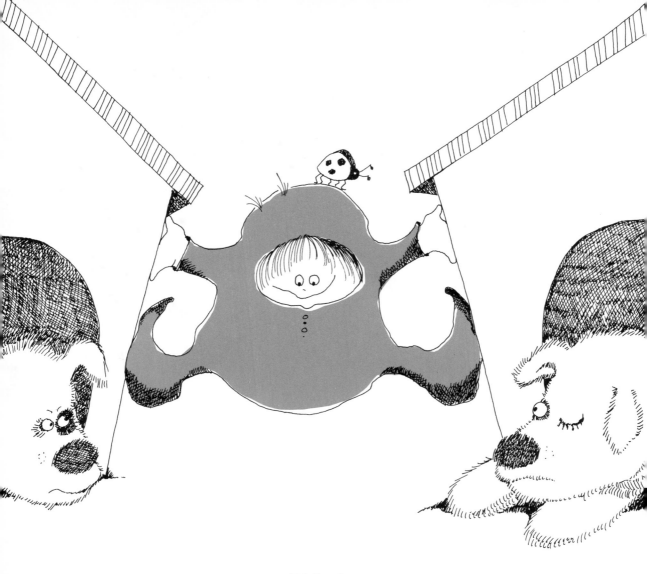

Wide

Narrow

Last

First

Straight

Crooked

BOOKS IN THIS SERIES

ANTONYMS
hot and cold and other
WORDS THAT ARE DIFFERENT
as night and day

MORE ANTONYMS
wild and tame and other
WORDS THAT ARE AS DIFFERENT IN MEANING
as work and play

STILL MORE ANTONYMS
together and apart and other
WORDS THAT ARE AS DIFFERENT IN MEANING
as rise and fall

HOMONYMS
hair and hare and other
WORDS THAT SOUND THE SAME
but look as different as bear and bare

MORE HOMONYMS
steak and stake and other
WORDS THAT SOUND THE SAME
but look as different as chili and chilly

STILL MORE HOMONYMS
night and knight and other
WORDS THAT SOUND THE SAME
but look as different as ball and bawl

HOMOGRAPHS
bow and bow and other
WORDS THAT LOOK THE SAME
but sound as different as sow and sow

HOMOGRAPHIC HOMOPHONES
fly and fly and other
WORDS THAT LOOK AND SOUND THE SAME
but are as different in meaning as bat and bat

British-American SYNONYMS
french fries and chips and other
WORDS THAT MEAN THE SAME THING
but look and sound
as different as truck and lorry

MORE SYNONYMS
shout and yell and other
WORDS THAT MEAN THE SAME THING
but look and sound
as different as loud and noisy

SIMILES
as gentle as a lamb, spin like a top, and other
"LIKE" OR "AS" COMPARISONS
between unlike things

MORE SIMILES
roar like a lion, as loud as thunder, and other
"LIKE" OR "AS" COMPARISONS
between unlike things

SOUND WORDS
jingle, buzz, sizzle, and other
WORDS THAT IMITATE THE SOUNDS AROUND US

MORE SOUND WORDS
munch, clack, thump, and other
WORDS THAT IMITATE THE SOUNDS AROUND US

PLURALS
mouse...mice, leaf...leaves, and other
WORDS THAT CHANGE IN NUMBER

POSSESSIVES
monkey's banana...monkeys' bananas,
thief's mask...thieves' masks, and other
WORDS THAT SHOW OWNERSHIP

LERNER PUBLICATIONS COMPANY
241 First Avenue North, Minneapolis, Minnesota 55401